Zion National Park

Animals & Attractions

Billy Grinslott & Kinsey Marie Books

ISBN - 9781960612861

There are many birds, reptiles and snakes in Zion Nationals Park. We have listed the larger animals that may be easier to spot and fun to see from a distance.

California condors are the largest birds in North America. They have a wingspans of 10 feet and weigh over 20 pounds. The California condor is estimated to live over 60 years. They are a weird looking bird and resemble the vulture. They can fly as high as 15 thousand feet.

Bald eagles live in just about every part of the world. The largest bald eagles tend to live in Alaska where they sometimes weigh as much as 17 pounds. They build the largest nest of any North American bird. The Bald Eagle is America's national bird. They return to the same nesting area every year.

The cliff chipmunk is small, and bushy tailed. It lives along cliff walls or boulders. Their stripes and face stripes are a little different than other chipmunks. Chipmunks are small members of the squirrel family. They have pouches inside of their cheeks so they can carry food. They are very friendly and will take food from your hand.

Rock squirrels live in burrows which they dig with their sharp claws and muscular legs. Unlike other squirrels they have adapted to living in treeless areas. They will climb trees if there is any in the area. Rock squirrels are one of the largest squirrel species. They grow up to a length of around 17 to 21 inches. Squirrels are important plant dispersers. They gather seeds and nuts and bury them in the dirt, which grows new plants.

This is a Gopher. Gophers are little excavators. They have sharp claws and make tunnels and burrows underground. That's where they live most of the time.

Porcupines have sharp quills on their backs to help protect them. A porcupine can have up to 30 thousand quills, they are sharp and will stick you if you touch them. To communicate they make grunts and high-pitched noises. A group of porcupines is called a family.

The Desert Tortoise is only found in the Mojave Desert in California, Nevada, Arizona, and Utah. Their Lifespan is 30-50 years, but some can live to be over 80 years old. These tortoises have stocky legs, perfect for crawling over rocky terrain. Desert tortoises are herbivores, dining on grasses, flowers, fruit, and cactus. These foods contain a lot of moisture, and desert tortoises can go for up to one year without access to fresh water.

Ringtails look like a racoon. They have stripes on their tails, but their face more resembles a cat. They are a member of the racoon family. Ringtails can be found in the south and southwestern parts of America. Ringtails are excellent climbers capable of ascending vertical walls, trees, rocky cliffs and even cactus. They are mostly nocturnal.

Gray fox prefers to live in rocky canyons and ridges but can also be found in wooded areas and open fields. They have strong, hooked claws that enable them to climb trees. Which is abnormal for a dog species. Gray foxes are not observed as frequently as red foxes due to their reclusive nature and more nocturnal habits.

The coyote is bigger than a fox. Eastern coyotes are part wolf. Coyotes are great for pest control. They like to eat mice and rats. They can adapt and live almost anywhere, even in the city. They have a yip type of call when they communicate with each other. Coyotes are found in all the United States, except Hawaii.

Bobcats are frequently misidentified as a lynx. Bobcats are part of the lynx family, but they are smaller than a lynx with different markings.

The mountain lion is one of the biggest cats in North America. The largest mountain lion ever recorded weighed 276 pounds. Mountain lions don't roar like other big cats they communicate in different ways, such as chirping, growling, shrieking, and even purring.

Mule deer get their name because of their mule like ears. Male deer are called bucks and females are does. Males grow new antlers every year. They can run 30 miles per hour. They are bigger than whitetail deer and prefer living in the mountain areas.

Desert Bighorn sheep are highly adapted for desert climates and can go for extended periods of time without drinking. They are social animals and form herds that are usually 8 to 10 sheep. Males will challenge each other and slam their heads together, that's how they got their name ram. Their horns can weigh up to 30 pounds.

Hwy 9 is the major road providing access to Zion National Park. It winds past the park visitor center and museum, and past many famous Zion landmarks. At any time of the year, you can drive through Zion National Park and the Zion-Mount Carmel Tunnel on State highway 9. Parking is limited along this road, but the views are incredible. It's a great drive, but it does not go into the park where the activities are.

Zion Canyon Scenic Drive. From March through late November, access to the Zion Canyon Scenic Drive inside Zion Park is by shuttle bus only. Private vehicles are allowed only when the Shuttle is not in operation. Bicycles are allowed on the Zion Canyon Scenic Drive, check with the park first. Zion Canyon Scenic Drive is approximately 7 miles long. The entire round-trip ride takes about an hour and a half. It stops at a few sightseeing opportunities.

The Narrows is the narrowest section of Zion Canyon. It has walls a thousand feet tall and the river sometimes just twenty to thirty feet wide, is one of the most popular areas in Zion National Park. A hike through the Narrows requires hiking in the Virgin River. You must get your feet wet since there is no trail.

Angel's Landing requires permits to take this hike. You must apply to a lottery system. It is one of the more popular hikes at Zion. But it is also dangerous. You are climbing 1,488 feet in elevation, up steep switchbacks. The part of the trail is along an exposed ridge, it is narrow and has chains to hang on too. As you can see in the lower right of the picture. This hike will test your fear of heights.

Canyon Overlook Trail is a moderate, 1 mile trail on the East side of Zion. The path begins with a series of sandstone steps with a metal handrails leading visitors over rocky terrain above a canyon. Near the end of the trail, the view opens to an expansive view of the canyon. At the end of the trail is a fenced cliff edge facing the main Zion Canyon, with excellent views of the Towers of the Virgin. Keep an eye out for bighorn sheep along the trail.

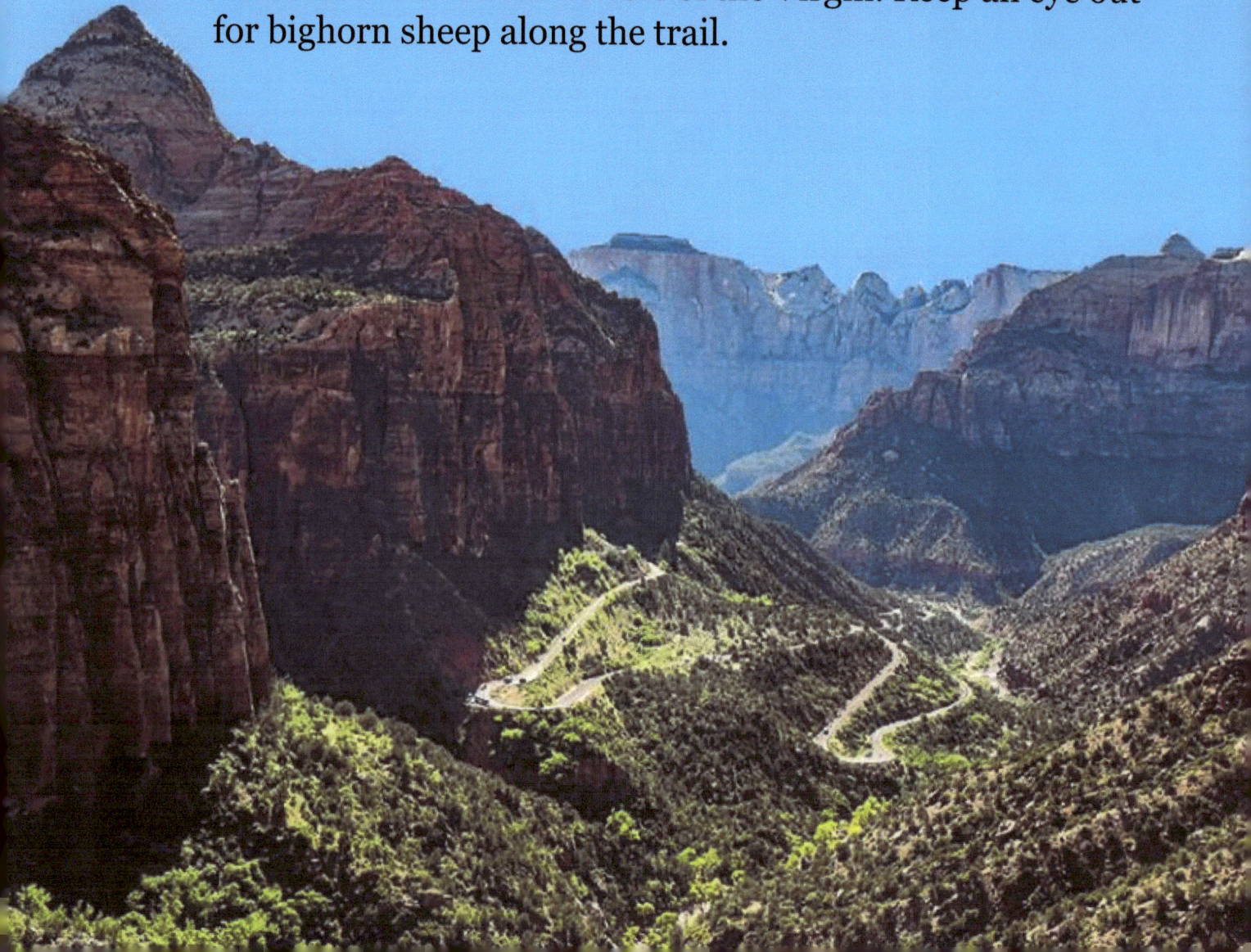

Observation Trail and Point. This short canyon leads hikers to the junction between the Observation Point Trail and the East Rim Trail. It is a narrow canyon, 1,100 feet above the Floor of the Valley Road. The trail follows along a shelf above the canyon floor. Below the trail, the canyon drops into an extremely narrow slot, which is a challenging technical route. A permit is required to descend Echo Canyon.

Zion Canyon is the most visited part of Zion and offers easy, moderate, and strenuous hikes. Most Zion Canyon hikes are accessible only by the park shuttle from March through November and require stopping at the appropriate shuttle stop. Be sure to check the shuttle schedule prior to starting your trip and arrive early to find parking

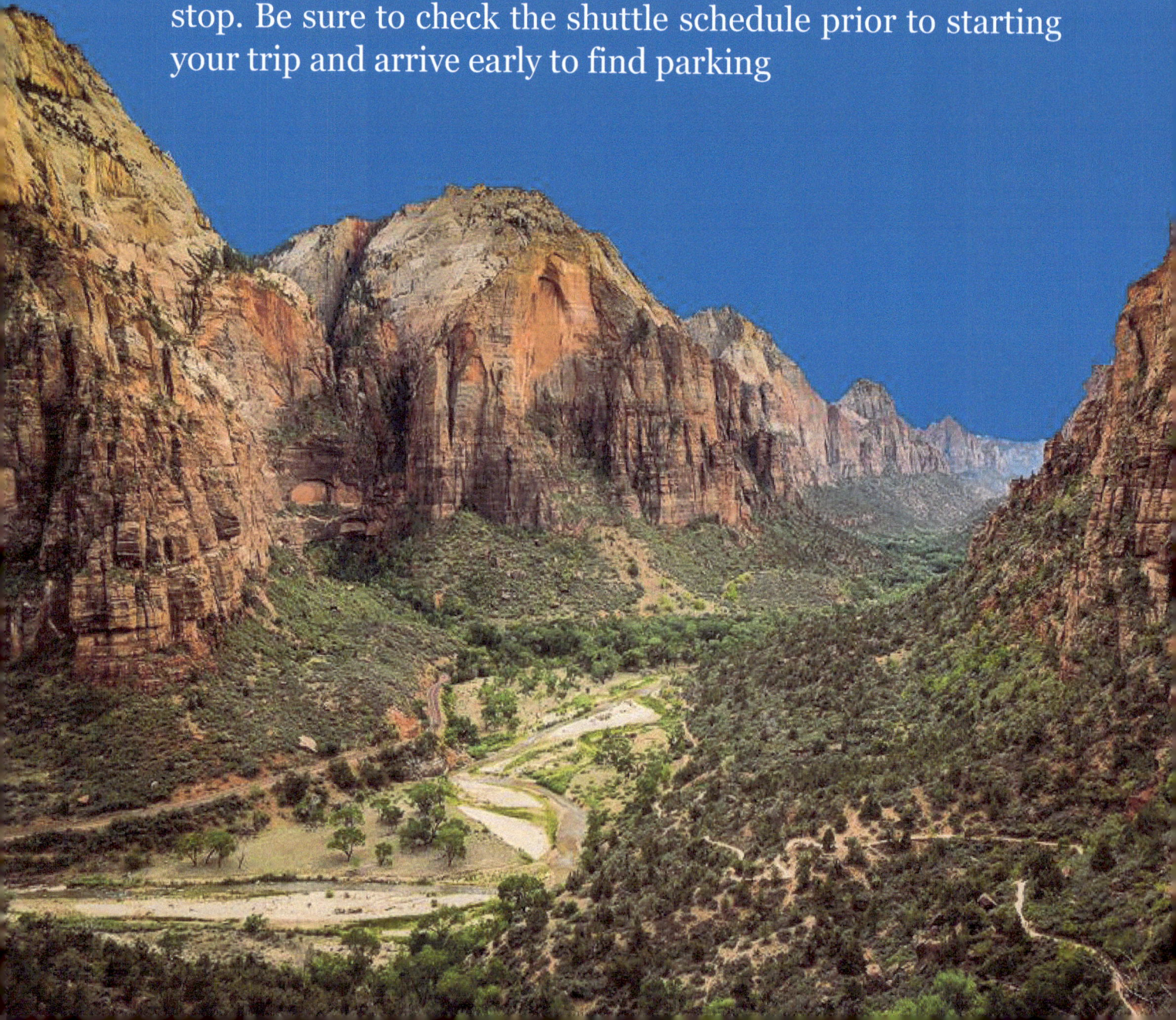

Canyon Junction Bridge. Access to the Canyon Junction Bridge in Zion National Park, take the Pa'rus trail leading from the Visitor Center. This bridge offers a great view of the mighty Watchman Mountain. This viewpoint is most popular at sunset. The bridge crosses the river and has great views all around.

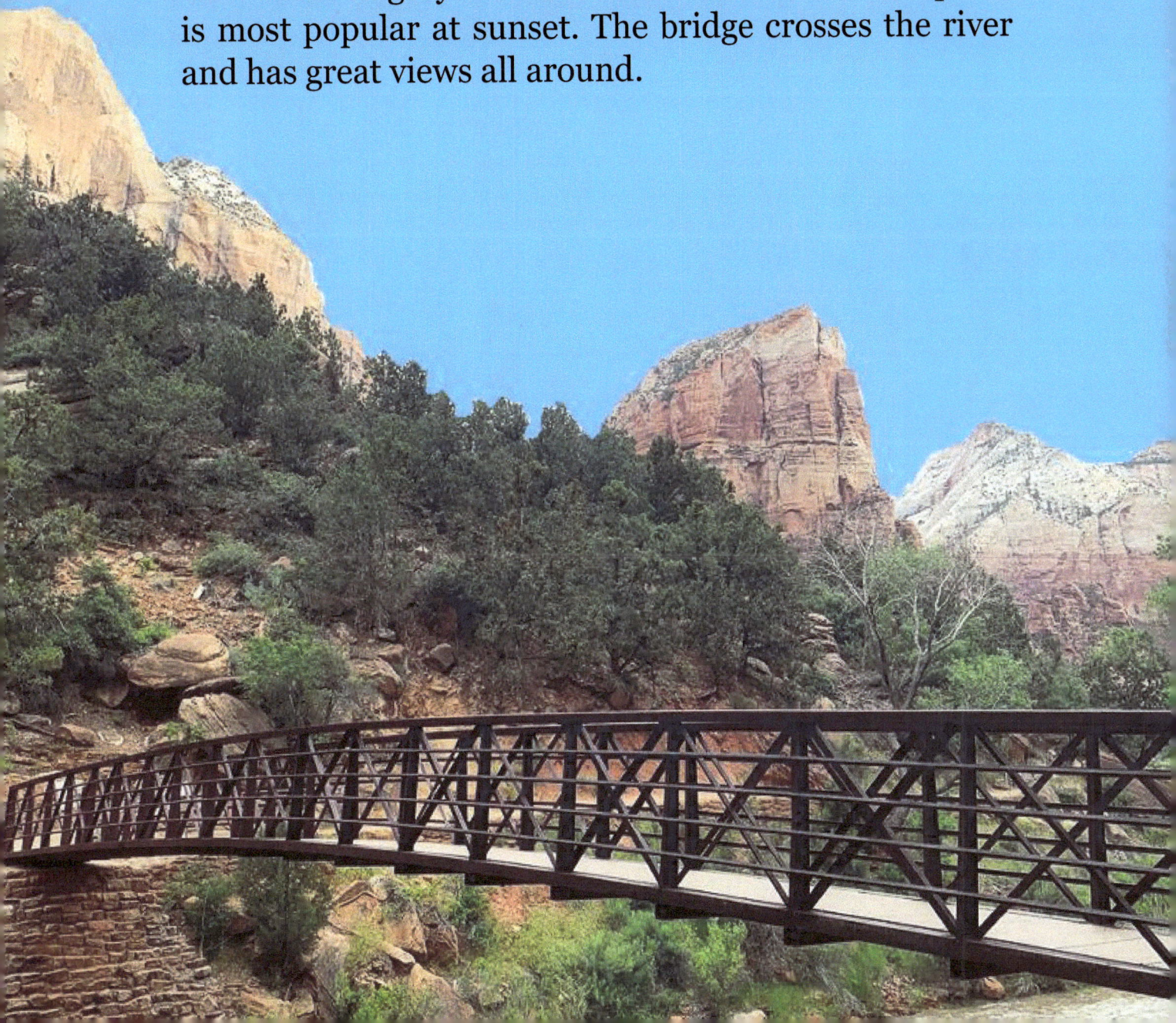

Weeping Rock is called that because water consistently runs out of the walls. Short but steep. From the parking area, you'll cross the bridge and head to the left onto a paved trail to Weeping Rock. The trail ends at a set of steps leading you to a rock alcove with dripping springs.

Kolob Canyon Road. A five-mile drive along the Kolob Canyons Road allows visitors to view the cliffs. It has access to other trails and scenic viewpoints. Located northwest of the Zion Canyon Visitor Center, Kolob Canyons is easily accessed off Interstate 15. It's well worth the trip.

Kolob Terrace Road. This is one of the best things to do in Zion National Park. Views from all sides of the car are amazing. There are plenty of areas to pull off and appreciate the park. Lava point is a breathtaking overlook, and there is plenty of space to have a picnic. Kolob Terrace Road runs from Virgin, Utah to Kolob Reservoir. The entire point-to-point route is about 25 miles.

The Kolob Canyons are a unique area of Zion National Park. It offers huge peaks of sandstone, canyon streams and cascading falls. It has over 20 miles of hiking trails. Kolob Canyon is home to one of the longest natural arches in the world. The Kolob Canyons are located at Exit 40 on Interstate 15, 17 miles south of Cedar City.

Zion-Mt. Carmel Highway. This scenic drive is worth it. If you drive from the canyon junction to the east, when you pass through the Zion-Mount Carmel tunnel (1.1 miles), you reach the trail head of Canyon overlook trail, you may hike the trail if you have time, otherwise, you can continue to drive the scenic drive. This 26-mile road winds its way eastward through some of the most exceptional terrain in the world.

The Riverside Walk is a relatively flat and paved 2.2-mile round-trip trail in the northern end of Zion Canyon. This easy walking trail follows the Virgin River as the tall cliff walls narrow in around you. The Riverside Walk is mostly flat through the first half-mile, although paving is irregular in some sections and minor drop-offs are present.

The Temple of Sinawava was carved by the Virgin River's incredible flow and power. To access this area, take the riverside walk trail ending at the Zion Narrows. Just one mile in length and paved over the entire route. The walk is as easy as a sidewalk stroll, making it perfect for everyone.

The Watchman Trail is a moderate out-and-back hike accessed from the Zion Canyon Visitor Center. If you climb up on watchman you will have a magnificent viewpoint of the Watchman, Temples and Towers, lower Zion Canyon, and the Town of Springdale. Watchman trail is 3.3 miles roundtrip.

The Subway is not for beginners. It is a technical slot canyon hike. To complete the hike, you wade, swim, scramble, and climb down the Left Fork of North Creek. The stream is the trail for most of the route. Some of the holes are deep enough that you have to swim, and the water is cold.

The Pa'rus Trail follows the Virgin River and has some of the best views of the Watchman. It is accessible for wheelchairs, pets on leashes, and bicycles. Along the way, the scenery is quite pleasant, including several bridges that cross above the river, various wildflowers, and mule deer can be spotted.

Court of the Patriarchs. Enjoy spectacular views of the three patriarchs, Abraham, Isaac, and Jacob. The three peaks are best seen from an overlook on the east side of the Zion Canyon Scenic Drive. The trail to the overlook is very short but steep. Also at this location you can enjoy excellent views of the Sentinel and Mount Moroni.

There are three Emerald Pools. Upper, Middle, and Lower in Zion National Park. Visitors may choose from as many trails: a short, 1.2-mile round-trip loop to the Lower Pool. A 2-mile round-trip visit to the Middle and Lower Pools. A 2.5-mile round-trip hike to all three. All Emerald Pool hikes lead to sparkling waterfalls and glistening pools.

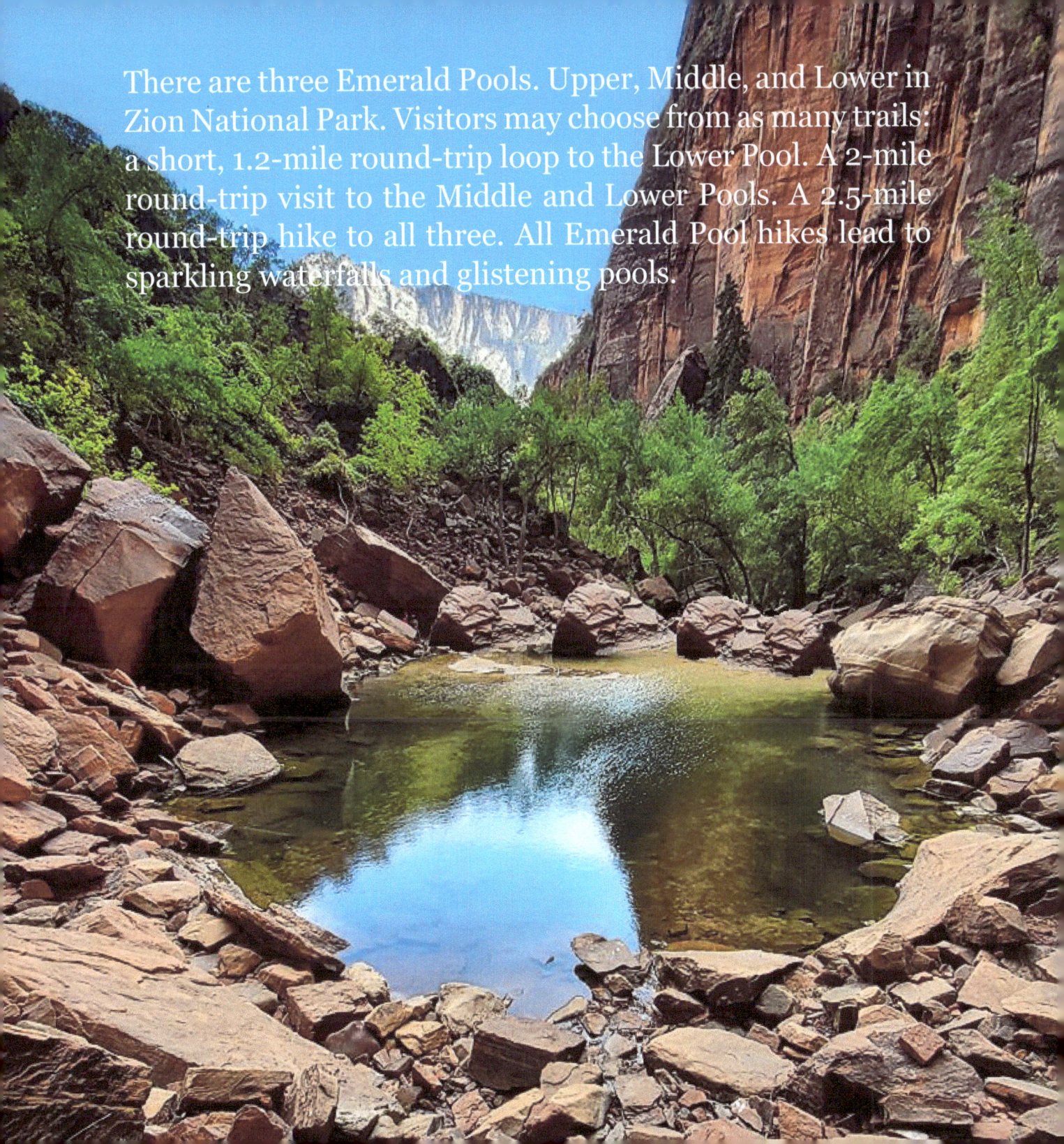

Taylor Creek, or Middle Taylor Creek, is a scenic hike in the Kolob Section of Zion National Park. The hike visits two historic cabins, as well as a deep walled canyon. The hike is very exposed to the sun to the first cabin, then gets a bit more shaded. The hike into the canyon is just over 2.5 miles long, rising just under 500 feet in elevation along its route.

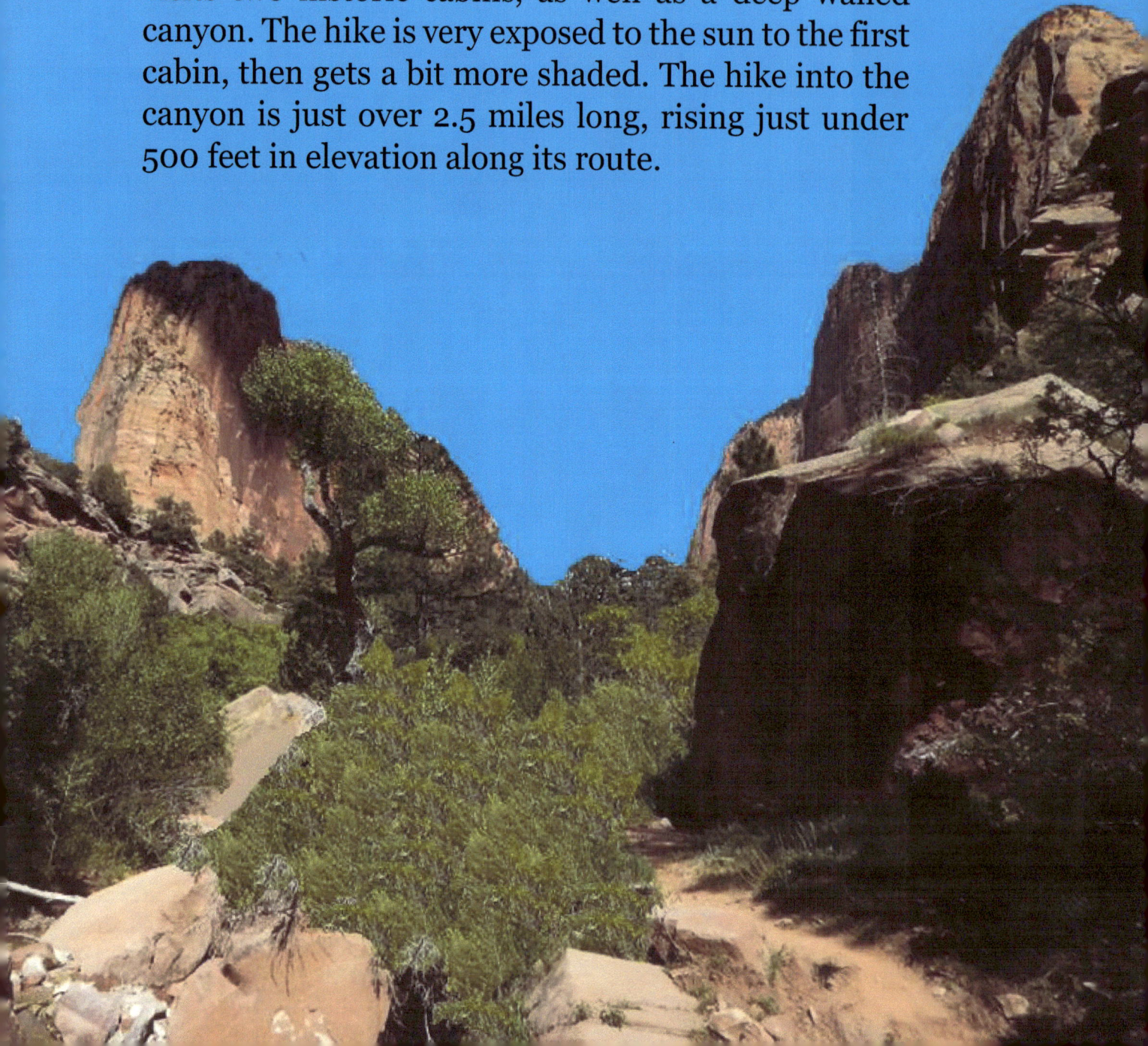

West Rim Trail. Fourteen miles of incredible scenery rivaling the best day hikes. From the West Rim Trailhead and through Potato Hollow, eventually rising 1200 feet onto the rim overlooking Great West Canyon, Phantom Valley, and Little Siberia down to Angels Landing. This is a great trail for camping overnight. It has plenty of campsites. You don't have to take the whole trail. You can turn around at any point. Day hikes are also available.

East Rim Trail. The trail heads up to the plateau with views of sandstone cliffs. A hike through ponderosa forest eventually leads to Stave Spring and the Deer trap and Cable Mountain. Or hikers can continue on the East Rim Trail and descend down into Echo Canyon towards Observation Point. The total trail is about 17 miles long. You can turn around at any point. Camping is also available.

Activities Available and Ways to Enjoy Zion

1. **Zion History Museum.** Take a free tour of the museum.

2. **Horseback Riding.** Guided trips are available.

3. **Hiking, Backpacking**. Enjoy walking through the trails.

4. **Biking.** Rent or bring your own bike.

5. **Birding.** Zion is home to 291 species of birds.

6. **Camping.** Zion has three campgrounds, need reservations.

7. **Canoeing, Kayaking, Rafting**, on the Virgin River.

8. **Ranger-led Activities**. Join a park ranger tour.

9. **Zion Shuttle.** Take a shuttle tour of the park.

Always Call and Plan Your Trip Before Going.

Author Page

Check Out More of Our Park and Kids Books

Billy Grinslott & Kinsey Marie Books

ISBN - 9781960612861

www.ingramcontent.com/pod-product-compliance
Lightning Source LLC
Chambersburg PA
CBHW060852270326
41934CB00002B/113